OVERCOMING
DISCOURAGEMENT

31 Keys To Bring You Freedom And Joy

Joe Garcia

Deeper Life Press

DEDICATION

I would like to dedicate this book to my great friend Rev. Melanie Hart.

Thank you for your love, support, encouraging words and beautiful smile.

Every time we talked in person, on the phone, through a text or even through video chat, you always had an encouraging word to say. You saw the best in everyone. Your words were always positive and full of faith, hope and love. Thank you for teaching me, and always pushing me to believe that *"all things are possible"*

Until your last breath you always believed, always hoped and always trusted. Even when it was very difficult for you physically, you did not allow discouragement to enter in. You stood firm on the word of God. Even during the times that I called or visited you to encourage you, it was I that would be encouraged by your words, your faith and your determination.

Today you are in heaven smiling down and cheering me on.

I love you dear friend.

Until we meet again

TABLE OF CONTENTS

A WORD FROM JOE GARCIA

Disappointments are Inevitable
Discouragement is a Choice

Like any Jewish man, Joseph, the Nazarene carpenter, looked forward to the day that was quickly approaching when he would take Mary as his wife and begin their life together. Then the shocking news came that she was pregnant....

Not many have experienced as bad a day as David did when he returned from a journey to his home in Ziklag and discovered that his enemies, the Amalekites, had plundered, destroyed or stolen everything that was important to him (1 Samuel 30). As David sat among the smoldering ruins of Ziklag and his men murmured against him and spoke of stoning him, he knew he had a choice. David could allow the overwhelming grief, distress and bitterness to conquer him so he would give up and quit. Or... he could encourage himself in the Lord, fight back and climb out of the black hole that was inviting him to fall into depression.

All of us face difficulties and disappointments in our lives. But we can have victory over them all if we keep our eyes on God and stay out of the mental/ emotional arena. We can imitate Joseph and David's responses in faith when we face unexpected difficulties by encouraging ourselves in the Lord, keeping our minds calm and taking encouragement from His Word even in the worst of times.

Everyone has known the difficulties, the sorrow, and the sadness that comes when life moves in surprising, unexpected directions. Disappointments may come as a result of a sudden change in circumstances, an abrupt reversal of your carefully laid out plans, or a challenging personal or financial issue. The exact cause of the change in the direction you were heading may be unknown. The dream you once cherished may seem to be lost and you may feel too overwhelmed to even know how to respond. It is often very difficult to sort through emotions when a sudden event seems to have come out of nowhere. If undetected, disappointments can lead to discouragement, which in turn can lead you to depression where you begin to believe the lie that you are worthless and helpless, and nothing will ever go right for you.

Emotional depression is probably the most common symptom of unhappiness in our world today. It affects rich and poor, men and women, young and old. Within one year 4 to 8 million are depressed to the extent that they cannot function effectively at their jobs. Suicide ranks as the fifth largest killer in the 15 to 55 age group. Over 80% of all suicide victims are deeply discouraged and depressed and most do not even know it.

In every case, it is a broken heart and a broken focus that comes from the destroyer of happiness and joy. That broken focus will slow you down, make you lose confidence and take the back seat, cause you to 'exist' and 'coast along', bring confusion and offenses, and most importantly will cause you to give up on God and take your focus off His promises.

Do you ever just feel tired, maybe exhausted or worn out? You may think its physical exhaustion but often it's due to an underlying, unresolved emotional disappointment that has led you to discouragement. A negative perception of your life's performance is a breeding ground for discouragement. There has simply been a disconnecting of who you were made to be, the real you, the spirit man or woman. You want to be on guard and watchful that you don't allow the disappointments of life to lead you into discouragement. As I said, discouragement, if you're not careful, can lead to depression.

As you begin moving into new territories with the Lord, you may experience some new and unfamiliar challenges: a relationship getting unusually difficult, a prolonged health condition you weren't expecting, a period of unemployment, etc. Discouragement may try to set in if you start losing your confidence and feeling hopeless about your future. It may seem like the troubling circumstances you're going through won't ever improve. But if you look beyond your circumstances to God, and stay in the realm of the Spirit, you'll discover the victory, the hope, the joy and the future He has promised you is still right there. I choose joy every day and I fight the enemy with it... and so can you!

Circumstances don't have to dictate your emotions! Circumstances don't change God's promises!

This is why I felt led to write this book. I want to help people overcome every obstacle of discouragement and experience the joy of the Lord... and how simple it can be to live in and enjoy the freedom found in that joy. We have overcome many things and I'm sure we will continue to encounter temporary roadblocks as we go higher with the Lord. But He will always be faithful to help us overcome them all with Wisdom from above and indescribable joy.

"The Lord is close to those who are of a broken heart, and saves such as are crushed with sorrow." Psalm 34:18, The Amplified Bible

"Your words have supported those who were falling; you encouraged those with shaky knees." Job 4:4, New Living Translation

Satan once put some of his tools up for sale in a garage sale. All of them were there: hatred, envy, jealousy, deceit, pride – each with an individual price tag. Off to the side was a harmlesslooking tool, well worn, but priced very, very high. One of the shoppers asked him what that tool was and why it was so expensive. "With a gleam in his eye, he responded proudly, "That's discouragement. It's more useful to me than all the others put together. I can pry open and get at someone's heart more deeply with discouragement than with any other tool. It's so worn out because I use it on almost everyone. And the best part is they rarely know it belongs to me."

~ Author Unknown

So do not throw away this confident trust in the Lord. Remember the great reward it brings you! Patient endurance is what you need now, so that you will continue to do God's will. Then you will receive all that He has promised.

Hebrews 10:35-36, New Living Translation

- DAY 1 -

PRAY - TALK TO GOD

God already knows how you feel, but He wants you to talk to Him about it and then listen for how the Holy Spirit guides you. Honestly vent your frustration and disappointment to God and keep in mind that He cares about what you're going through. "Is prayer our steering wheel or our spare tire?" Throughout your life prayer should be the first and last resort in all circumstances. Thank Him for deliverance from circumstances that aren't His will, and perseverance to empower you to endure circumstances that are His will. When it comes to talking to God about something, we should not pray, "If it be His will." We already have God's promise in His Word. It is His will that our needs are met and that we are healed. We read in Mark 11:24 AMP, *For this reason I am telling you, whatever things you ask for in prayer [in accordance with God's will], believe [with confident trust] that you have received them, and they will be given to you.* When we pray He will help us realize it is His will that all our needs are already met — spiritual, physical, and material.

'Call to Me and I will answer you, and tell you [and even show you] great and mighty things, [things which have been confined and hidden], which you do not know and understand and cannot distinguish.' Jeremiah 33:3, AMP

Praying always with all prayer and supplication in the Spirit. Ephesians 6:18a, KJV

Then if my people who are called by my name will humble themselves and pray and seek my face and turn from their wicked ways, I will hear from heaven and will forgive their sins and restore their land. 2 Chronicles 7:14-15, NLT

CHANGE YOUR ATTITUDE

You can begin today to work on changing your attitude toward the present problem or situation. Even though you may not be able to change the circumstances in which you work or live, you can always change your attitude. God will do the rest. God calls His people to be transformed by the renewing of their minds. This transformation of thinking God's thoughts is a daily pursuit. Your improved attitude will also change the way you talk about it... causing you to speak words of life over the atmosphere surrounding your circumstances. A change in attitude will minister to those around you who have been very concerned about you.

And do not be conformed to this world [any longer with its superficial values and customs], but be [a]transformed and progressively changed [as you mature spiritually] by the renewing of your mind [focusing on godly values and ethical attitudes], so that you may prove [for yourselves] what the will of God is, that which is good and acceptable and perfect [in His plan and purpose for you]. Romans 12:2, AMP

Regarding your previous way of life, you put off your old self [completely discard your former nature], which is being corrupted through deceitful desires, 23 and be continually renewed in the spirit of your mind [having a fresh, untarnished mental and spiritual attitude], 24 and put on the new self [the regenerated and renewed nature], created in God's image, [godlike] in the righteousness and holiness of the truth [living in a way that expresses to God your gratitude for your salvation]. Ephesians 4:22-24, AMP

- DAY 3 -

ASK FOR HELP

You can receive help from those who are close to you if you're not afraid to ask. These may be family, friends, neighbours and church members, and those who love you the most who are there to help if you're not afraid to ask! Asking for help reveals your strength, not your weakness. If you've ever shied away from asking for help because of fear that you may seem weak, you aren't alone. It is sad that during the times we need to ask for help that most people remain silent. We can do so much more together than we can ever do alone. Too often we try to 'tough it out' rather than reaching out to ask for help when we need it. Fear and pride may try to get the better of us while depriving others of a chance to show they care and share their gifts.

And I will do whatever you ask in My name [[a]as My representative], this I will do, so that the Father may be glorified and celebrated in the Son. John 14:13, AMP

As iron sharpens iron, So one man sharpens [and influences] another [through discussion]. Proverbs 27:17, AMP

TRUST

I have learned how necessary it is to develop a more powerful and complete trust in the Lord; we simply need a fresh encounter with God and His Word. Believe and trust that His words are true and that they are for you. He will accomplish His will through you, as you trust Him. You may have a hard time being able to trust anyone as a result of some great disappointments from either teachers, preachers, parents or spouses. But faith and trust go hand in hand. First you must have faith that God exists, that He is who the Bible says He is, and that you are truly saved under the shed Blood of His Son Jesus Christ. Once you are saved, then you must be willing to surrender fully your entire life (and your discouraging circumstances and situations) over to God the Father so He can then enter you into His perfect plan and manifest His destiny for your life. You must become both saved and surrendered, not just saved. This is how to trust in the darkest of times.

Trust in and rely confidently on the Lord with all your heart And do not rely on your own insight or understanding. Proverbs 3:5, AMP

When I am afraid, I will put my trust and faith in You. Psalm 56:3, AMP

- DAY 5 -

EXCHANGE

Learn to exchange a lust for the world for the Kingdom of God. People try to deal with discouragement in many wrong and destructive ways. Many plunge themselves into other things they think will bring them fulfillment: entertainment, sports, travel, careers or even ministry. Tragically, some turn to the world of drugs or alcohol. These things only dig you deeper into the world of discouragement. A few become so discouraged and depressed that they take their own lives.

The kingdoms of this world tell you to ignore God, that He is not that important and isn't involved with your problems, concerns or affairs. So, don't pay much attention to God, the world says. Take matters into your own hands!

The Kingdom of God says that God is supremely important. Your reason for being is to exist for God, to love Him, seek His presence, serve Him, and worship Him. In everything you do, glorify God and He will always be with you. Everything that you do, say, and think should represent Him, and bring Him honor. Don't ignore God but exchange your disappointments for His joy.

But first and most importantly seek (aim at, strive after) His kingdom and His righteousness [His way of doing and being right—the attitude and character of God], and all these things will be given to you also. Matthew 6:33, AMP

You have changed my sadness into a joyful dance; you have taken away my sorrow and surrounded me with joy. Psalm 30:11, Good News Translation

- DAY 6 -

GOD'S VOICE

When you are discouraged, the thing that will most refresh you is to hear God speaking to you and your particular circumstance through His audible voice or through His Word. Set time to read the Word daily. I have often found that the Scripture I am reading each day has particular relevance to the very circumstances I am going through at the time. Because God most often communicates through His Word, you need to read it and read it and read it. You will benefit greatly from the Holy Spirit's power in it and your faith will rise! Don't neglect God's voice you will also hear through your pastor. Stay in fellowship with your church family and those you trust who can speak hope into your life. One word from God can change everything! His voice is all that matters!

Therefore everyone who hears these words of mine and puts them into practice is like a wise man who built his house on the rock. Matthew 7:24, NIV

My son, if you receive my words and treasure up my commandments with you, making your ear attentive to wisdom and inclining your heart to understanding; yes, if you call out for insight and raise your voice for understanding, if you seek it like silver and search for it as for hidden treasures, then you will understand the fear of the Lord and find the knowledge of God. Proverbs 2:1-5, English Standard Version

- DAY 7 -

NO COMPARISONS

It's easy to think that you're doing okay in the Lord if you compare yourself to others. We always seem to compare ourselves to those who aren't quite as committed as we see ourselves. But then you come to God's Word, and it exposes the thoughts and intentions of the heart. You realize that God wants purity in your thought life. He calls you to love Him first with all your heart, soul, mind, and strength. The Word shows how we need to adjust our thinking, our priorities, and our behavior to please God, and not others, and to be the unique individual He created us to be. To overcome discouragement, we need a fresh encounter with God and a fresh revelation of who we really are... one of a kind, a peculiar treasure. Your destiny depends on the unique part of you and not the part of someone else you may be trying to be like. You are perfect - God stopped at perfection, you are God's masterpiece.

For we are His workmanship [His own master work, a work of art], created in Christ Jesus [reborn from above—spiritually transformed, renewed, ready to be used] for good works, which God pre-pared [for us] beforehand [taking paths which He set], so that we would walk in them [living the good life which He prearranged and made ready for us]. Ephesians 2:10 AMP

We do not dare to classify or compare ourselves with some who commend themselves. When they measure themselves by themselves and compare themselves with themselves, they are not wise. 2 Corinthians 10:12, NIV

For you are a holy people, who belong to the Lord your God. Of all the people on earth, the Lord your God has chosen you to be His own special treasure. Deuteronomy 7:6, NLT

RELINQUISH SELF--PITY

Relinquish self-focus and self-pity by letting go of your hurts. Often self-focus generates self-pity and self-justification for why we quit serving the Lord or why we give up on hope. With Elijah, we might begin to say, *"I have been very zealous for the Lord, but everyone else has forsaken Your covenant, torn down Your altars and killed Your prophets... I alone am left; and they seek my life, to take it away."* (1 Kings 19:10). That kind of self-focus prevents us from recognizing and ministering to the needs of others and keeps us out of faith. This is a serious and dangerous place to be in. It is our responsibility to take off what no longer belongs to us and put on our new self.

I have been crucified with Christ [that is, in Him I have shared His crucifixion]; it is no longer I who live, but Christ lives in me. The life I now live in the body I live by faith [by adhering to, relying on, and completely trusting] in the Son of God, who loved me and gave Himself up for me. Galatians 2:20, AMP and put on the new self [the regenerated and renewed nature], created in God's image, [godlike] in the righteousness and holiness of the truth [living in a way that expresses to God your gratitude for your salvation]. Ephesians 4:24, AMP

- DAY 9 -

BE BOLD

One way to persevere in the face of opposition is to give a bold, strong witness of our faith in Jesus Christ. Our words and declarations commit us so that we know others will be watching. If we will be bold for the Lord, we can know that His eye is upon us in whatever response our enemies come back with. Be bold enough to let everyone know you believe God's words and that they are true.

I have learned a simple but very profound statement from my friend Joshua Mills; "believe the Word of the Lord on purpose", it's a small but powerful truth. His Word is true, believe it and stand on it. If God brought you to it He will bring you through it, so be bold and very courageous, know that He is with you every step of the way.

Jesus states in John 14:26 *"But the [a]Helper (Comforter, Advocate, Intercessor—Counselor, Strengthener, Standby), the Holy Spirit, whom the Father will send in My name [in My place, to represent Me and act on My behalf], He will teach you all things. And He will help you remember everything that I have told you."* The Holy Spirit will direct you as you seek to walk in the light of God. As you surrender to Him you will see the uncommon favor of the Lord, but you MUST be VERY BOLD and VERY COURAGEOUS.

What is Courage? Mr. Webster says: it is the ability to do something that frightens one. Strength in the face of pain or grief. The ability to control your fear in dangerous or difficult situation, to be brave and confident enough to do what you believe.

Remember, you are not alone in your quest, for the Spirit of Truth will guide you. Believe His Word on purpose, He as not changed His mind. Just because in the natural it does not make sense it does not mean He is not with you.

Learn to shut all the other voices out and learn to lean and believe the promises of God over your life. He's got your back.

May God bless you with the courage to face the future with hope, confidence and unspeakable joy. May you be full of His Glory as you walk daily in His abundant mercies, as He reveals His truth to you. If God is for you , who can be against you?

To be more than conquerors means we face the trials of life with the certainty that we are not alone. We have a mighty Father who fights for us. We approach the darkest valleys with confidence, knowing that nothing can happen to us that has not been permitted by our loving Father for our good.

We have this promise that "He will never leave us", we have His word. Don't draw back, be bold and very courageous, knowing that you are not facing any situation alone. Your God is with you it is His presence that guarantees your success.

Have I not commanded you? Be strong and courageous! Do not be terrified or dismayed (intimidated), for the Lord your God is with you wherever you go." Joshua 1:9 AMP

Yet in all these things we are more than conquerors and gain an overwhelming victory through Him who loved us [so much that He died for us]. Romans 8:37 AMP

REMEMBER WHO GOD IS

The things you focus on you will empower.

What are you focusing on? In the natural it might not make sense, your feelings might be telling you otherwise, and as you look through the natural eyes things don't seem to add up. Remember "you should not allow your feelings to lead you" the Spirit of truth, the Spirit of God is the one that should be leading you. Tell your feelings to submit to the Spirit of God that is in you.

Shift your focus from your discouraging circumstances over to Almighty God Himself. He can change a situation in the blink of an eye! Remember that He is love, and also that He is all-powerful. Trust that God will surely help you because that's the consistency and faithfulness of His character. He is the supernatural Lord of your breakthrough.

Shift your focus to His promises, and stand on them, believe them with all your heart and don't let the natural situations lead you. His word is true and He does not change, He is the same yesterday, today and forever. He takes pleasure in your prosperity, He loves you and He is on your side.

God is Just - Acts 17:31

God is Loving - Ephesians 2:4

God is Truthful - John 14:6

God is Holy - 1 John 1:5

God is Compassionate - 2 Corinthians 1:3

God is Merciful - Romans 9:15

God is Graceful - Romans 5:17

God is Forgiving - Psalm 130:4

With God we will gain the victory, and he will trample down our enemies. Psalm 108:13 NIV

The LORD says to my lord: "Sit at My right hand until I make your enemies a footstool for your feet." Psalm 110:1, NIV

Wealth and honor come from you alone, for you rule over everything. Power and might are in your hand, and at your discretion people are made great and given strength. 1 Chronicles 29:12, NLT

STICK TO YOUR ASSIGNMENT

Think and pray about the work you're currently doing and how your life is going. Ask Him to clarify whether or not He has truly led you to your current assignment. Reflect on the successes and failures you've experienced so far and see if you can recognize a pattern that can help you discern if you're doing what you should be doing. If it seems as if you're doing what God wants you to do but you just need to overcome some challenges while doing it, then stick with it and don't give up! Instead, fight discouragement by writing down a fresh vision for how to continue your work in the future by eliminating the stress.

Remember He has a specific assignment for you. It's not a decision you make, rather it is a discovery of God's plan for your life.

Don't allow discouragement or negative words to slow you down. People might not fully understand what your assignment is, but you do because He called you to it. Surround yourself with people that will encourage you and help you get there. Believe God and stick to your assignment, but remember that believing in God means that you will obey him, stay focus and push through.

For I know the plans and thoughts that I have for you,' says the Lord, 'plans for peace and well-being and not for disaster, to give you a future and a hope. Jeremiah 29:11 AMP

And whatever you do or say, do it as a representative of the Lord Jesus, giving thanks through him to God the Father. Colossians 3:17, NLT

Let the favour of the Lord our God be upon us, and establish the work of our hands upon us; yes, establish the work of our hands! Psalm 90:17, English Standard Version

- DAY 12 -

GOD'S PERSPECTIVE

God sees your future as clear as this: *"Blessed is the man who perseveres under trial, because when he has stood the test, he will receive the crown of life that God has promised to those who love him"* (James 1:12). That's a great promise and it's for us because it's what God sees and God never changes! God's perspective comes from Heaven. If you're frustrated your perspective may be coming from earth. Align your life with God, and see what He sees. This will keep you walking in faith without wavering.

Remember, God knew the ending before we even saw the beginning. He can work every moment of our lives for our good, according to His purpose for us. Continue to ask God for Heavenly vision, with eyes to see. Let Him guide you step by step to the destination He has planned for you.

As you behold Him, you will fulfill His plan and you will be shaped more and more into His image!

And we know [with great confidence] that God [who is deeply concerned about us] causes all things to work together [as a plan] for good for those who love God, to those who are called according to His plan and purpose. Romans 8:28 AMP

After this time had passed, I, Nebuchadnezzar, looked up to heaven. My sanity returned, and I praised and worshiped the Most High and honored the one who lives forever. His rule is everlasting, and His Kingdom is eternal. Daniel 4:34, NLT

Where there is no vision [no revelation of God and His word], the people are unrestrained;

But happy and blessed is he who keeps the law [of God]. Proverbs 29:18, AMP

- DAY 13 -

GIVE TO PEOPLE IN NEED

Reaching out to help others will be encouraging for you, because it will give you back the joy of knowing that God is still using you in significant ways, in spite of your circumstances. Reaping always follows sowing. We will discover that we have often forgotten how blessed we actually are! I have learned that by serving and giving to others, not only do we help them, but we put our own problems in a fresher perspective. When we concern ourselves more with others, there is less time to be concerned with ourselves. In the midst of the miracle of serving, there is the promise of Jesus, that by losing ourselves, we find ourselves. Our passion to love should be the foundation for our giving.

It is not how much we give, but how much love we put into our giving.

Whoever finds his life [in this world] will [eventually] lose it [through death], and whoever loses his life [in this world] for My sake will find it [that is, life with Me for all eternity].

Matthew 10:39, AMP

Give generously to him, and do not let your heart be grieved when you do so. And because of this the Lord your God will bless you in all your work and in everything to which you put your hand. Deuteronomy 15:10, Berean Study Bible

- DAY 14 -

CHOOSE FAITH OVER FEAR

Recognize that the love of God is always with you, even in the middle of the most discouraging circumstances. Whenever we feel afraid, choose to trust God despite the fear. When we begin to imagine what else could go wrong... we're not in faith. Choosing faith in the face of fear stretches us to grow up spiritually. God may not change our circumstances the instant we'd like Him to, but He has given us the faith we need to deal with them as long as necessary and not a minute longer. Remember that faith pleases God, especially when we're in a battle with fear. We were given the victory 2000 years ago, so by choosing the Word of God, we can make the choice to choose faith over fear.

Fear is a Liar. It is your worst enemy. The attitude that every believer should have is "I will not fear". Fear is the enemies favorite tool that he has to use against believers. Fear is not from God, the enemy uses it against us so he can hold us back - and stop us in our tracks. He wants to hold you back so that you won't obtain all that God has created for you. There has been times in all of our lives that fear has stopped us from crossing over, from taking that leap of faith, or stepping into your breakthrough. He has held you back from investing in things, applying for that job, making that business deal, trusting that person or even trusting the word of God. Scriptures say that we have been set free from fear. Deuteronomy 31:8 says *"He will never leave you nor forsake you. Do not be afraid; do not be discouraged"*.

Remember , being set free from something does not mean the disappearance of it. From time to time in your life, you will have fear come against you. Fear will tempt you, but just because it will come and knock at your door does not mean you have to let it in and give it a place in your mind and heart. Yes it will try to come at you, but you will recognize it and you will have an option; am I going to allow it to control me or do I have control over it? If you don't make the decision to not allow fear in, you will give room for the enemy to come in where he will rob, kill and destroy.

Resist the enemy, don't put up with fear, don't give room to it. He can only do what you give him permission to do.

"What, then, shall we say in response to these things? If God is for us, who can be against us?

Romans 8:31

Think about this scripture. If God is for you, what difference does it make who is against you? If God is for you, believe it in your heart. He is not for you because you are good, He is for you because He is good.

"The Lord is on my side i will not fear"

Psalm 18:6

See, God is on your side because He loves you. He will not love you more tomorrow than He loves you at this exact moment, is because He loves you unconditionally.

No matter where you come from, no matter where you are, no matter what you will do, God loves you. His love for you is unconditional, His love for you is perfect.

He says in His word that "perfect love casts out fear". Fear not, as you know and experience His perfect and unconditional love. You will have the courage to encounter fear and press into what God has for you. So remember, the Lord is on your side, "FEAR NOT"

You see that [his] faith was working together with his works, and as a result of the works, his faith was completed [reaching its maturity when he expressed his faith through obedience]. James 2:22, AMP

God is our refuge and strength [mighty and im-penetrable], A very present and well-proved help in trouble. Therefore we will not fear, though the earth should change. And though the mountains be shaken and slip into the heart of the seas, Though its waters roar and foam, Though the mountains tremble at its roaring. Psalm 46:1-3, AMP

- DAY 15 -

PERSEVERANCE

Change requires perseverance. It may not happen overnight but God honors loving obedience and faith that can persevere over time. And the reward for enduring is a crown of life. God promises deep fulfillment and rich joy beyond your wildest dreams in this lifetime. When you come through your trials, you begin to experience His joy. If you've ever met a patient, caring, wise person who radiates the love of Jesus, I can almost guarantee that he or she has suffered and persevered at some point in their life. The way God produces that kind of person is through adversity. They don't give up, the life of Christ begins to manifest through them, and they have a strong inner joy and fulfillment from God that cannot be touched or moved by circumstances.

Mr. Webster says that perseverance is; persistence in doing something despite difficulty or delay in achieving success.

Delay does not mean denied. If you are in a time of delay, just remember that God is at work on your behalf, and you will see His breaththrough as you continue to persevere. It's in the moments of delay that we must understand and realize that we have a loving God that is at work on our behalf behind the scenes. He is always working and always creating; just trust Him and trust His timing.

God delays because His ways are not your ways.

"For my thoughts are not your thoughts, neither are your ways my ways declares the Lord. As the heavens are higher than the earth, so are my ways higher than your ways and my thoughts than your thoughts" Isa. 55:8-9

God's ways are higher. Trust that he has a divine purpose for His delay. Your viewpoint is limited, but God sees all things. Proverbs 3:5 says, *"Trust in the Lord with all your heart and lean not on your own understanding."* God may be putting everything in place before revealing His answer to you.

God delays so you can demonstrate your faith.

Galatians 6:9 tells you how to wait for God: *"Let us not become weary in doing good, for at the proper time we will reap a harvest if we do not give up."*

Respond to God's delay with faith, not doubt. God guarantees a harvest, and it will arrive at the proper time. Hebrews 10:36 says, "You need to persevere so that when you have done the will of God, you will receive what he has promised."

To persevere is to endure with an expectation of victory. Stand firm and expect that the thing that He promised you He will deliver. Your victory is on its way.

And let endurance have its perfect result and do a thorough work, so that you may be perfect and completely developed [in your faith], lacking in nothing. James 1:4, AMP

He only is my rock and my salvation; My fortress and my defense, I will not be shaken or discouraged. Psalm 62:6, AMP

- DAY 16 -

GET RID OF CARNAL EXPECTATIONS

When you make a change for the better, you expect things to start improving immediately. Many people suddenly find themselves in an overwhelmingly difficult situation and begin praying, going to church, studying the Word, and overhauling their lifestyle. And when they've stuck with it for a week, or a month and nothing seems to be changing, they feel like they've gotten a raw deal and their faith begins to waver. Never mind that they've been sowing bad seeds into a career or a family situation for twenty or thirty years. Most of us feel that if we've made the right changes, we expect to see the right consequences happen pretty soon. And while God does mercifully work that way, He doesn't always. Sometimes the fruit of our obedience takes a little more time to grow into real faith. Let Him deliver you His way, in His time.

The lame man looked at them eagerly, expecting some money. Acts 3:5, NLT

Then they set out from Mount Hor by the way of the [branch of the] Red Sea [called the Gulf of Aqabah], to go around the land of Edom; and the people became impatient, because [of the challenges] of the journey. Numbers 21:4, AMP

- DAY 17 -

RESIST THE TEMPTATION OF DEPRESSION

Remember the Bible's promise that if you resist Satan, he will flee from you. Every day, thank God for the spiritual insight and strength you need to fight the attacks you encounter in this fallen world. When the world tries to deceive you and you feel confused, pray to discern the truth. When adversaries try to bring divisions between you and others, make every effort to keep the unity of the Holy Spirit through the bond of peace. Fight back with the Truth of His Word! Discouragement is a choice. If you feel discouraged, it's because you've chosen to feel that way. No one is forcing you to feel bad. Hang on! Do what's right in spite of your feelings. No feeling lasts forever. My favourite saying is... "I choose joy every day and I fight the enemy with it." You can too.

"...And do not be worried, for the joy of the Lord is your strength and your stronghold."

Nehemiah 8:10b

The Lord is near to the heartbroken

And He saves those who are crushed in spirit (contrite in heart, truly sorry for their sin). Psalm 34:18, AMP

I waited patiently and expectantly for the Lord; And He inclined to me and heard my cry. He brought me up out of a horrible pit [of tumult and of destruction], out of the miry clay, And He set my feet upon a rock, steadying my footsteps and establishing my path. He put a new song in my mouth, a song of praise to our God; Many will see and fear [with great reverence] And will trust confidently in the Lord. Psalm 40:1-3, NIV

USE THE GIFTS GOD GAVE YOU

What are you really good at? Painting? Counseling? Maybe you are a great mechanic or you're an amazing chef. Perhaps you just find opportunities to help people wherever you go. Whatever your talent or skill is, guess what? God's behind it! But He didn't bless any of us with a talent or skill simply so we could look awesome or earn lots of cash.

God wants us to steward those gifts for Him! Maybe you thought stewardship was just for your money. Well, yes, that's a big part of it. But it's so much bigger than that. Stewardship is about everything in our lives—and that includes our talents.

If we want to please God—if we want to hear Him say, "Well done good and faithful servant" when we meet Him in heaven—then we must faithfully use our talents the way He wants us to.

Letting your gifts and talents lie dormant will only increase a sense of hopelessness and discouragement.

Ask God to lead you to specific situations where you can put them to full use for God's glory, and to help make the world a better place. Your gifts are for sharing and you can give your way out of trouble. Remember that the 'circumstance' called Goliath gave David the opportunity to use his faith, his gifts and his talents that made him a king!

Colossians 3:23–24 (ESV) tells us that everything we do should be for Christ: *"Whatever you do, work heartily, as for the Lord and not for men, knowing that from the Lord you will receive the inheritance as your reward. You are serving the Lord Christ."*

Just as each one of you has received a special gift [a spiritual talent, an ability graciously given by God], employ it in serving one another as [is appropriate for] good stewards of God's multi-faceted grace [faithfully using the diverse, varied gifts and abilities granted to Christians by God's unmerited favor]. 1 Peter 4:10, AMP

Since we have gifts that differ according to the grace given to us, each of us is to use them accordingly: if [someone has the gift of] prophecy, [let him speak a new message from God to His people] in proportion to the faith possessed; Romans 12:6, AMP

SHARE YOUR FAITH WITH OTHERS

Whenever God gives you the opportunity to share your faith with others who are seeking Him, do so with gladness. If we follow the way of love, we team up with an unstoppable force. You'll remind yourself of how God has worked in your life and you'll experience the joy of helping others discover Him. Sharing your testimony will bring you hope, as well as hope to a hurting, lost and lonely world. One of the best ways to share your faith is to demonstrate the very things you believe by staying in faith, doing what you say and having a good attitude even in the middle of a crisis in your own life. You can be the face of Jesus to the world.

As you share your faith with others, I pray they may come to know all the blessings Christ has given us. Philemon 1:6, Contemporary English Version

Love one another. As I have loved you, so you must love one another. By this everyone will know that you are my disciples, if you love one another. John 13:34-35, NIV

- DAY 20 -

SIMPLIFY YOUR LIFE

One way to simplify your life is to not waste time on being negative. We all have things that happen to us that turn the day from good to bad. Maybe your car wouldn't start in the morning, a friend cancelled on you at the last minute, or you got a negative review at work. Having a negative reaction to these types of things is only natural, but it's what you do in these situations that can really impact your life. If you find that you are spending the rest of your day thinking about how bad these things are, you are wasting your time. Yes, it is really that simple.

Like I said, that immediate reaction is a natural part of coping. However, instead of dwelling on the negatives that may be occurring in your life, such as feeling regret and/or gossiping, you can be more productive by using this time for things that actually matter. Moving past difficult things is, just that, difficult, but finding ways to refocus your energy will help you get through your day and life in general.

Just think about how much time you may have wasted recently by dwelling on the negative and thinking about the "what-ifs" in a situation? Being more positive and finding ways to move past bad situations is a hard but important way to simplify your life.

The Word of God tells us in Philippians 4:8 to zoom in, center your mind on the things at are from above and implant them in your heart.

Finally, [a]believers, whatever is true, whatever is honorable and worthy of respect, whatever is right and confirmed by God's word, whatever is pure and wholesome, whatever is lovely and brings peace, whatever is admirable and of good repute; if there is any excellence, if there is anything worthy of praise, think continually on these things [center your mind on them, and implant them in your heart]. Philippians 4:8 AMP

Base your schedule on your priorities. Learn to make yourself the number one priority. Don't waste time and energy on activities that don't reflect what's most important to you; this causes stress and anxiety. Stress is deadly. Stress can intensify what makes a person depressed without them even knowing it. Freeing yourself from unnecessary tasks will encourage you and give you time to rest peacefully. It will give you time to gain insight and understanding into the situation. Thinking of your own well-being before others is not a popular teaching but a necessary one, to simplify your life and learn to live stress free and love more! Keep life simple.

Peace I leave with you; My [perfect] peace I give to you; not as the world gives do I give to you. Do not let your heart be troubled, nor let it be afraid. [Let My perfect peace calm you in every circumstance and give you courage and strength for every challenge.] John 14:27, AMP

But the Lord said to her, "My dear Martha, you are worried and upset over all these details! There is only one thing worth being concerned about. Mary has discovered it, and it will not be taken away from her." Luke 10:41-42, NLT

- DAY 21 -

SPEND TIME WITH OVERCOMERS

The Bible has a lot to say about being an overcomer. The term overcomer is especially prominent in the book of Revelation, where Jesus encourages His people to remain steadfast through trials. 1st John 5:4–5 says, *For [a]everyone born of God is victorious and overcomes the world; and this is the victory that has conquered and overcome the world— our [continuing, persistent] faith [in Jesus the Son of God]. Who is the one who is victorious and overcomes the world? It is the one who believes and recognizes the fact that Jesus is the Son of God.*

Overcomers are followers of Christ who successfully resist the power and temptation of the world's system. An overcomer is not sinless, but holds fast to faith in Christ until the end. He does not turn away when times get difficult or become an apostate. Overcoming requires complete dependence upon God for direction, purpose, fulfillment, and strength to follow His plan for our lives. "Find your tribe" is a saying that people would often use when trying to encourage someone to find those that are like minded. On the journey to being an overcomer and no longer being discouraged, you will need to find overcomers that you can surround yourself with.

Time in a person's positive presence will naturally make us feel better ourselves. Serving as a mentor brings many rewards, and can help to take our eyes off any situation. Surrounding ourselves with victorious overcomers will lift us up, bring answers, impart wisdom, change the atmosphere and help us to fly like eagles. Be cautious and careful to choose wise counsel so you don't receive pity but instead receive supernatural Heavenly solutions instead.

He who walks [as a companion] with wise men will be wise, But the companions of [conceited, dull-witted] fools [are fools themselves and] will experience harm. Proverbs 13:20

My son, keep your father's command and do not forsake your mother's teaching. Proverbs 6:20, NLT

TAKE CARE OF YOUR BODY AND HEALTH

Giving your body the care it needs, will help you feel less discouraged and stronger in the long run. Eat a healthy diet, exercise regularly, soak up the sun and get enough sleep. Consuming toxic-laden foods and drinks will keep you in a 'fog' and from seeing clearly. Begin to eliminate the temptation to sleep less, overeat, consume sugary processed foods with too much salt. Taking care of yourself must become a priority and cannot be stressed enough. The resurrection of Jesus Christ removed the limitations from the body, the temple and house of the Holy Spirit. It is our responsibility to keep the body in order for God to use us in mighty ways. Dreams and visions will become an everyday occurrence, joy will return, and you will love your newfound energy.

I discipline my body like an athlete, training it to do what it should. Otherwise, I fear that after preaching to others I myself might be disqualified. 1 Corinthians 9:27, NLT

Do you not know that your bodies are temples of the Holy Spirit, who is in you, whom you have received from God? You are not your own; you were bought at a price. Therefore honor God with your bodies. 1 Corinthians 6:19-20, NIV

- DAY 23 -

A FORGIVING HEART

You may have every reason to be offended but you have no right! Look inward and immediately start the cleansing process. The wise and the happy person removes first the impurities from within. The longer the poison of resentment and unforgiveness stays in a body, the greater and longer lasting is its destructive effect. As long as we blame others for our condition or circumstance and build a wall of self-justification around ourselves, our strength will diminish and God's power and ability to help us rise above the situation will fade away. The poison of revenge, or of unforgiving thoughts or attitudes, unless removed, will destroy the soul. The Lord said He would forgive and forget the sins of those who have truly repented. Oftentimes we choose to decide when we think a person has repented, and when we will forgive. But God says the time is ripe for your healing and breakthrough is through a forgiving heart!

Guard your heart above all else, for it determines the course of your life. Proverbs 4:23, NLT

God blesses those whose hearts are pure, for they will see God. Matthew 5:8, NLT

If you forgive others the wrongs they have done to you, your Father in heaven will also forgive you. But if you do not forgive others, then your Father will not forgive the wrongs you have done. Matthew 6:14-15, Good News Translation

- DAY 24 -

THIS IS TEMPORARY

The myth about the future is that your situation "will always be this way." If your job has always been terrible, you'll eventually embrace the lie that it always will be. The same goes for a marriage, a home, parents, children, or whatever struggle comes along. However, the truth is that it won't last forever! Discouragement falsely interprets the past and present as an unbreakable pattern, which can lead to even more discouragement and even depression. If you want to see life from God's perspective, you have to reject the thought that this season is permanent. Anything not coming from God — you have the authority over! As a child of God you are seated in limitless eternity at the right hand of God. You are no longer locked into the realm of time where you're limited to constraints, lies and boundaries that hinder His promises. God will take you from Glory to Glory if you see things are about to shift!

To every thing there is a season, and a time to every purpose under the heaven. Ecclesiastes 3:1, KJV

Jesus replied, "It is not for you to know times or seasons that the Father has fixed by His own authority. Acts 1:7, Berean Study Bible

WORRY IS NOT FAITH

God is not unaware of our needs, and since He has committed Himself to providing them for us, why should we worry about them? If we trust in God to provide for our needs, then we must let Him do it in His time and in His way. Worry is thinking about the same problem over and over. Worry never works, never solves problems, and never changes circumstances. There is no need to become trapped in a lifestyle of worry. You see, just as worry is a foe of faith, faith is also a foe of worry!

It isn't difficult to understand how worry and his brother fear could be faith killers. Those who have extreme fear about anything will naturally focus on themselves and the problems they are facing, not on God and His willingness to help them in their time of great need. The cure for worry is trusting God. Remain in faith, resist the enemy and expect answers and a turn-around to suddenly appear!

Can any one of you by worrying add a single hour to your life? Matthew 6:27, NIV

Give all your worries and cares to God, for He cares about you. 1 Peter 5:7, NLT

- DAY 26 -

WATCH YOUR WORDS

Did you know that what you said yesterday has become your today? You can receive your answers, your healing, your breakthrough... and live the abundant, healthy life God has always planned for you if you watch your words. Keep them in line with God's words by speaking God's promises each and every day. God's Word, taken daily like medicine, believed in your heart, and spoken out your mouth is health to your spirit, soul and body! You are a co-creator with Christ. "He ruined my life!" "My back is killing me." "She'll never forgive me." Think before you speak because every word is going into the atmosphere and creating either life or death for you and those around you.

Those who guard their mouths and their tongues keep themselves from calamity. Proverbs 21:23, NIV

Death and life are in the power of the tongue,

And those who love it and indulge it will eat its fruit and bear the consequences of their words. Proverbs 18:21, AMP

- DAY 27 -

HIS PRESENCE IS YOUR HOPE

Because you know that God is good and is able to work all things together for your good, you can find the strength of heart to continue on. He will not leave you or let you down no matter how fiery or painful your trial is. His presence will always bring you hope. His Word is true and His joy is your strength. Since your hope is in Him, don't neglect His presence. Discouragement has a unique way of either keeping us connected to Him... or disconnecting us from God's presence, our life's source. It is easy to forget how much we need God when the skies are blue, the sun is shining and the birds are singing. But when we watch the dark clouds roll in and the storms come, that's when we must choose to seek shelter in Him... our connection to an abundant life.

The presence of God is not a place where you visit on a sunday morning or when you pray worship or even when you at a church service. The presence of

God is a place, where we need to learn to live from and not visit. You are a carrier of His presence, learn to work, breath, worship, walk, sing, preach and live from His presence. When you choose to live from His presence life will flow from you and nothing will be impossible to you. His presence is your vital need!

When you pass through the waters, I will be with you; and when you pass through the rivers, they will not sweep over you. When you walk through the fire, you will not be burned; the flames will not set you ablaze. Isaiah 43:2, NIV

But as for me, it is good for me to draw near to God; I have made the Lord God my refuge and placed my trust in Him, That I may tell of all Your works. Psalm 73:28, AMP

You reveal the path of life to me; in Your presence is abundant joy; at Your right hand are eternal pleasures. Psalm 16:11, NLT

- DAY 28 -

RELINQUISH GUILT

Below are symptoms of guilty feelings for both real and imaginary guilt. Their force may vary from person to person. It's merely a basic list of signs associated with possible lingering feelings of guilt. Guilt will keep you from overcoming discouragement and keep you tied to your present circumstances. Guilt and all of the toxic symptoms must be dealt with and released quickly. You were forgiven and set free at the cross with Jesus' blood and the powerful resurrection. Receive what He purchased for you by releasing any or all of these listed below. God wants you free to soar!

1. *Nervousness*

2. *Depression*

3. *Defensiveness*

4. *Suspicion of others*

5. *Sleeplessness, insomnia*

6. *Fear, panic attacks*

7. *Escapism, fight*

8. *Insecurity*

9. *Judgmentalism*

10. *Lack of concentration*

11. *Shallow friendships*

12. *Blaming others*

13. *Self-contempt, self-denigration, self-condemnation*

14. *addictions , self-destructive behavior*

He himself bore our sins in His body on the tree, so that we might die to sins and live for righteousness; by His wounds you have been healed.

1 Peter 2:24, English Standard Version

But [in fact] He has borne our griefs, And He has carried our sorrows and pains; Yet we [ignorantly] assumed that He was stricken, Struck down by God and degraded and humiliated [by Him]. But He was wounded for our transgressions, He was crushed for our wickedness [our sin, our injustice, our wrongdoing]; The punishment [required] for our well-being fell on Him, And by His stripes (wounds) we are healed. Isaiah 53:4-5, AMP

WATCH OUT FOR FATIGUE

When you're physically or emotionally exhausted, you could be out of the will of God and a prime candidate to be infected with discouragement. Your defenses are lowered, your immune system is down and things can seem harsher than they really are. This often occurs when you're trying to accomplish a pressure-filled situation without God. If you need a break then take one! You'll be more effective when you return rested and back in the center of His will, seeing your circumstances like He does. If you're 'burning the candle at both ends', you're not as brilliant as you thought! Remember: fatigue is an enemy of love.

Come to Me, all who are weary and heavily burdened [by religious rituals that provide no peace], and I will give you rest [refreshing your souls with salvation]. 29 Take My yoke upon you and learn from Me [following Me as My disciple], for I am gentle and humble in heart, and you will find rest (renewal, blessed quiet) for your souls. Matthew 11:28-29, AMP

For those who receive that rest which God promised will rest from their own work, just as God rested from his. Hebrew 4:10, Good News Translation

- DAY 30 -

CHOOSE JOY – FIGHT THE ENEMY WITH JOY

Well, we all have not so good days don't we? We all get discouraged at one time or another.

One tool that I use everyday to fight the enemy with is JOY!!! Joy is a choice, choose today to be joyful.

Now, I am not so naive to think that we will always be on the top of the world and having mountain top experiences, for there will be occasions that we will have to travel through the valleys and deserts for a while. However, neither am I so spiritually ignorant that I am not aware of how God has provided for us in times of those valleys and deserts experiences.

In this life we will have tribulation.

In this life we will have trouble

In this life we will have difficulty

In this life we will have trials, sickness and hard times. The storm will rise, the winds will blow, the waves will crash against your life. There will be discouragement, things won't go as planned, sorrow, weeping, financial difficulties, dark days and uncertain times.

BUT the thing that God has provided for us in the hard times of this life is JOY!!!!

Psalm 30:5 (NLT) - *For his anger lasts only a moment, but his favor lasts a lifetime! Weeping may last through the night, but joy comes with the morning.*

Isaiah 61:3 (NIV) - *and provide for those who grieve in Zion—to bestow on them a crown of beauty instead of ashes, the oil of joy instead of mourning, and a garment of praise instead of a spirit of despair. They will be called oaks of righteousness, a planting of the LORD for the display of his splendor.*

What is JOY? Mr. Webster says: it is the emotion evoked by well-being, success or good fortune or by the prospect of possessing what one desires.

Joy is a strong feeling of happiness; a manifestation of happiness through an outward rejoicing or excitement.

To the people who don't know Jesus those definitions might be true. However, to the Christian (someone who should know Jesus) something different applies as it relates to OUR joy.

This outward rejoicing comes from an inward satisfaction that I know Jesus Christ, that I know He is in control and all will be well.

JOY IS A CHOICE - CHOOSE TO FIGHT THE ENEMY WITH JOY EVERYDAY

The Joy of the Lord is your strength. Yes, our strength is limited, but the Lord's strength has no limitations. The Lord's strength is unlimited, and forever strong. He is the same yesterday, today and forever.

Are your financial resources limited? Perhaps so, but we serve an unlimited God that holds all resources and takes pleasure in your prosperity and that includes your finances as well.

Can your health falter, and leave you physically weak? Of course it can and perhaps it has. The Lord's strength, however, is perfect and complete. Our confidence in God is, at times, the only strength we know.

So, our JOY is knowing that no matter what comes our way - whether it's personal hardship for us or our family - or maybe just the routine ups and downs, good times and bad times or simply times of both strength and exhaustion - through it all, we have a relationship with a God whose strength is overwhelming and limitless.

Because of that, WE HAVE JOY.

Your enemy is after your joy. He knows if he steals your joy, he will have your strength.

If he makes you focus on the negative, the problem, the situation that is impossible for you to resolve, he will steal your joy and when he steals your joy he will steal your strength.

Remember, the thing you focus on is the thing you will empower!

In all that we face, we have a choice. Choose to focus on God's promises, and don't focus on the impossible. Choose Joy.

Consider it nothing but joy, my [a]brothers and sisters, whenever you fall into various trials. Be assured that the testing of your faith [through experience] produces endurance [leading to spiritual maturity, and inner peace]. And let endurance have its perfect result and do a thorough work, so that you may be perfect and completely developed [in your faith], lacking in nothing.

James 1:2-4 (AMP)

- DAY 31 -

NEVER GIVE UP!

Keep holding on to God's promise that He has a very important plan for your life. God never changes His mind. Everything that you need or want is already in your life, just waiting for Him to reveal it, for you to recognize it and then receive it. Expect Him to show you your destiny! No matter how old or young you are, or what you're going through, you're destiny will never change. God promises greater things are in store for you — a future filled with promise and hope! You must never give up. Keep on the path. Keep on walking. You may need to just change your sight to that which is Heavenly and you will receive a reward when this trial is finished. You'll get a fulfilling, abundant life on this earth in communion with Him, and you'll receive an eternal heavenly crown if you understand that God sees you as victorious. Discouragement will become an old, worn-out tool never to be used on you again. Keep on seeking and knocking. And remember... never give up!

Brothers, I do not consider myself yet to have laid hold of it. But one thing I do: Forgetting what is behind and straining toward what is ahead, I press on toward the goal to win the prize of God's heavenly calling in Christ Jesus.

Philippians 3:13-14, Berean Study Bible

Have I not commanded you? Be strong and courageous! Do not be terrified or dismayed (intimidated), for the Lord your God is with you wherever you go." Joshua 1:9, KJV

Develop success from failures. Discouragement and failure are two of the surest stepping stones to success." ~ Dale Carnegie

"Discouragement is not the absence of adequacy but the absence of courage." ~ Neal A. Maxwell

AN UNENDING FLOW

God dispenses His goodness not with an eyedropper but with a fire hydrant. Your heart is like a coffee cup, and His grace is the Mediterranean Sea. You simply can't contain it all, so let it bubble over. Spill out. Pour forth. And enjoy the flood of His greatness that helps you overcome every situation. You can fight every enemy with joy so let it bubble up from deep within. Receive the unending flow right now of exactly what you are needing in your life. It is really God's love for you, despite your shortcomings and failures that enables you to overcome. He continues to pour Himself out and fill you with His overflowing love. It's that overflowing love that you want to turn your attention to right now.

See how very much our Father loves us, for He calls us His children, and that is what we are! But the people who belong to this world don't recognize that we are God's children because they don't know Him. 1 John 3:1-2, NLT

For I will pour out water to quench your thirst and to irrigate your parched fields. And I will pour out my Spirit on your descendants, and my blessing on your children. Isaiah 44:3, NLT

PRAYER

I'm often surprised at how easy it is to feel like I'm falling short in every area of my life. And even if I am falling short, I know I live under God's goodness and His grace. My close family and friends offer me constant grace, as well.

That's how I know it's the enemy and not the truth. He wants to keep me discouraged so I stay focused on myself and not on Jesus.

So, I'm going to God in prayer and if you're discouraged, you may want to join me...

Almighty God, I exalt and worship Your Holy name. I am so grateful for every time You've encouraged and lifted me up. You are the faithful One. You are the ever-powerful One. You are the merciful One.

You know how I react to the discouraging thoughts launched at me by the evil one. Forgive me for focusing on myself more than on You. May the anointing on this book be an instrument of Honor that brings me into His Glorious Joy, Rest, and Freedom.

You've commanded me to be strong and courageous and to trust You as my shield and defender. You've proven over and over that You use the weak things to display Your unlimited Power and Wisdom. I need these valuable truths to move me beyond my head and into my spirit. The fear of Discouragement is a hurdle I want to learn to quickly jump over. I know I will never be a slave to the trauma and discouragement of yesterday when I have Your Joy.

I want to overcome Discouragement, be bold in faith, bold in hope, and full of joy and love. Father, my hope is in You! I trust You, confident that Your grace, mercy, and love cover every evil effort that works to defeat and discourage me. You are my strength and shield. You give me countless reasons to rejoice. The Holy Spirit lives big in me to display His Glory to those He died to save.

Make me an instrument of His life-changing victory! Teach me to live in the joy and freedom You've so graciously provided through the blood of Jesus and the precious Holy Spirit. Open my ears to Your promptings. Fill me so completely with Your unconditional love for others that I speak as You inspire me without even the slightest hesitation. Empower me to pray for others with a listening, compassionate ear trusting that You will always show me and anoint me in what to pray.

Use me to awaken those who are numb to Your love. Let Your Words of life flow through me to those who may be resisting You.

Revive, restore and resurrect me so that with my life You can revive, restore and resurrect others.

In Jesus' Name, I pray...believing, receiving and trusting. Amen

MEET THE AUTHOR

Joe Garcia is the lead pastor of The River International Church, an apostolic center located in Hamilton, Ontario, Canada. You are invited to worship with Joe and Bella Garcia every Sunday at 10:00 AM (EST), or watch the live services online on The River International Church Facebook page or YouTube channel.

The River International Church
1221 Wilson St. East
Hamilton, ON - L8S 4K6 - Canada
www.theriverinyou.com

Joe & Bella have been married for 29 years and have 3 children: Andrew, Joel and Rachel. Together they are business owners, revivalists and lead pastors. They have ministered in many nations of the world, including Mozambique, Brazil, Trinidad and Tabago, the USA, Portugal, Bulgaria and Sri Lanka. Their purpose is to passionately and intentionally pursue the Presence of God, equip the saints, and rise up leaders and world changers. They move in the prophetic, and carry a breaker anointing with a contagious spirit of revival and joy. Joe is also the leader of the Ontario Prophetic Council.

Joe and Bella Garcia are working book projects including a book for children. Their first book released is a beautiful 31-day devotional, "Igniting Your Day", available on Amazon and Kindle. As you arise and shine, read these daily chapters, and quote these declarations you will begin to experience an igniting and an infusing of the power of God's Word in your life (A Deeper Life Press publication)

Joe's latest book "Catapulted" will help you to skillfully navigate the process of your journey. In this book Joe invites you to join him as he reveals the success secrets God has lovingly imparted, instructed, and accomplished through him seeking Him during the challenging processes, continual transitions, and the often, unfamiliar seasons of his journey with Him. As God guided him and taught him how to say "YES", in order to partner with His plan to make the transition process peaceful and successful. (A Deeper Life Press publication)

Dear Reader,

If your life was touched while reading *"Overcoming Discouragement"*, please let us know!

We would love to celebrate with you!

Please visit our website,

www.glorycarriersinternational.com

www.theriverinyou.com

Spreading Glory Fires from **The River** to **the Ends of The Earth,**

Joe & Bella Garcia

info@glorycarriersinternational.com

"Igniting Your Day"

31 Days of Declarations To Ignite The Power Of God's Word In Your Life

Joe & Bella Garcia

Available on Amazon and Kindle or through on our online store

www.glorycarriersinternational.com

"Catapulted"

Skillfully Navigating The Process Of Your Journey

Joe Garcia

Available on Amazon and Kindle or through on our online store

www.glorycarriersinternational.com

Contact Joe Garcia on

Facebook: Joe Garcia, Bella Garcia

Instagram: pjgarcia & bellag777

Twitter: @pjgarcia7 & Bgarcia777

"A Presence-Driven Publisher"

www.deeperlifepress.com

52064757R00056

Made in the USA
Middletown, DE
07 July 2019